D1403467

ONE MINUTE
AFTER YOU DIE

STUDY GUIDE

ERWIN W. LUTZER

MOODY PUBLISHERS
CHICAGO

Scripture quotations are from the ESV® Bible (The Holy Bible, English Standard Version®), copyright © 2001 by Crossway, a publishing ministry of Good News Publishers. Used by permission. All rights reserved.

Developed by Dana Gould
Interior design: Erik M. Peterson
Cover design: Smartt Guys design
Cover image of supernova copyright © Masterfile / 679-02684646. All rights reserved.

ISBN: 978-0-8024-1296-6

We hope you enjoy this book from Moody Publishers. Our goal is to provide high-quality, thought-provoking books and products that connect truth to your real needs and challenges. For more information on other books and products written and produced from a biblical perspective, go to www. moodypublishers.com or write to:

Moody Publishers
820 N. LaSalle Boulevard
Chicago, IL 60610

1 3 5 7 9 10 8 6 4 2

Printed in the United States of America

CONTENTS

INTRODUCTION

This study guide is to be used with the book and DVD series, both of which are titled *One Minute After You Die* by Dr. Erwin Lutzer (available from Moody Publishers).

This guide is intended for both individual and group use. When used in a group setting, this guide will be helpful for both the group leader and the participants who wish to read the relevant sections of the book and respond to the DVD presentations together. It might also be helpful to take notes or to begin considering the questions in each section while watching the DVD.

Although the content of the book and the DVD series

are essentially the same, there are some differences in the order the material is presented. For this reason, each set of study questions begins by giving specific information as to what parts of the book should be read in preparation for the DVD lecture and the questions to follow.

Simply read the section in the *One Minute After You Die* book labeled **please read**, and you will be prepared for both the lecture and the questions below.

WHO CAN TELL WHAT LIES ON THE OTHER SIDE?

In preparation for these discussion questions and the DVD lecture, **please read:**

CHAPTER 1, *"Attempting to Peek behind the Curtain"*

CHAPTER 2, *"The Descent into Gloom"*

From the Author

Denial, anger, fear, depression, and helpless resignation—all these feelings erupt in the hearts of those who face death. No matter that death is common to the human race; each person must face it individually. No one can endure this moment for us. Friends and family can walk only as far as the curtain; the dying one must disappear behind the veil alone.

Naturally, we would like to know in advance what we can expect on the other side. Human nature being what it is, we grasp for some clue, some hint we might glean from those who are about to cross the boundary.

7

Reincarnation, altered states of consciousness, and glad reunions in a metaphysical place such as heaven are popular themes at the box office. Dozens of movies portray the enchantment of the life beyond. Fear of death has been supplanted by blissful feelings about a hereafter where everyone ends happily reunited. There is no judgment, no careful review of one's life. To be sure, death has mystery, we are told, but it is not to be dreaded.

How legitimate are reported glimpses from behind the curtain? Many are convinced that the immortality of the soul is now confirmed by paranormal experiences that can have no other explanation than that the soul does survive the death of the body. But can reliable information be transmitted back to earth by those who tell us what they have seen and heard from the other side?

Although we have no reason to think that we can peer behind the curtain and report what we have found, we can gratefully accept all that God has shown to us in His Word.

ENGAGING THE TOPIC

Answer these questions while watching the DVD and reading the book.

1. Life's last great mystery is death. We must all face this mystery _____ .

2. Those who engage in the occult practice of channeling claim they are speaking with the_____.

3. Followers of the doctrine of reincarnation hold that death itself does not _____ .

4. Usually, near-death experiences involve a person's soul being separated from their _____ .

5. Near-death experiences may not reflect the _____ experiences of life beyond death.

6. Authoritative and reliable information about what exists beyond death comes to us only from what God reveals to us in the _____ .

QUESTIONS FOR DISCUSSION

1. What personal experiences can you share as you think about the topic of death? Do you fear death or do you welcome it?

2. What are some dangers channeling presents to its practitioners? How do demonic spirits influence this activity?

3. Read Deuteronomy 18:11–12 and Isaiah 8:19–20. What do these passages tell us about God's view of one's consulting a medium?

4. From a biblical point of view, how may we explain the phenomenon of ghosts? What should be our position regarding this phenomenon?

5. Discuss the doctrine of reincarnation. What are its basic premises?

6. Discuss 2 Corinthians 11:14 and Satan's practice of duplicating God's light by disguising himself as "an angel of light." What other deceptions and substitutions for truth might we find within these occult practices?

7. Discuss the qualifications of Jesus in telling us what lies on "the other side."

8. Describe your understanding of the concept of *sheol*. How would you explain your view to someone?

9. What Greek word is used in the New Testament to translate the Hebrew *sheol*? What do you think the story Jesus told in Luke 16 teaches us about the afterlife?

PERSONAL REFLECTION

For the believer in Christ, we have a glimpse beyond the curtain, and it is based on the authoritative Word of God. Christ has risen from the dead and in doing so has conquered death. We can have no greater assurance regarding death than from the risen Christ: "I died, and behold I am alive forevermore, and I have the keys of Death and Hades" (Revelation 1:18).

If you are a Christian, you may rejoice that death is not an enemy to be feared. The apostle Paul declares in 1 Corinthians 15:55, "O death, where is your victory? O death, where is your sting?" The sin that gave death its sting has been conquered by our Lord (vv. 56–57).

We may go about our walk of faith, confidently anticipating death. As Paul wrote to the Corinthian church: "We know that while we are at home in the body we are away from the Lord, for we walk by faith, not by sight. Yes, we are of good courage, and we would rather be away from the body and at home with the Lord. So whether we are at home or away, we make it our aim to please him" (2 Corinthians 5:6–9).

Even so, death has mysteries that must be explored. In the next section, we will discuss what unbelievers experience at death.

ENGAGING THE TOPIC answers:

1. Alone 2. Dead 3. Exist 4. Body 5. True 6. Bible

WHAT DO UNBELIEVERS EXPERIENCE WHEN THEY DIE?

In preparation for these discussion questions and the DVD lecture, **please read:**

CHAPTER 2, *"The Descent into Gloom"*

From the Author

Death, we must remember, is the consequence of Adam and Eve's disobedience in the garden of Eden. God had warned them that if they ate the forbidden fruit, they would die. And die they did. They died spiritually in that they were separated from God and tried to hide from Him. They also began to die physically, as their bodies had begun the journey to the grave. And if Adam and Eve had not been redeemed by God, they would have died eternally, which is the third form of death. From the original disobedience in Eden, death in all its forms began its trek throughout the world.

As we learned in the last session, the most important word in the Old Testament that speaks of the afterlife is the Hebrew word *sheol*. So here are some facts we should know in order to understand what the Old Testament means by the word *sheol*. First, there is a clear distinction between the grave, where the body rests, and sheol, where the spirits of the dead gather. Second, sheol is often spoken of as a shadowy place of darkness, a place that is not part of this existence. Third, after death one can be united with his ancestors in sheol.

In the New Testament, we find *sheol* translated by the Greek word *hades*. The New Testament pulls back the curtain so that we can see into hades (or sheol) with more clarity. Here we are given some very specific details about what hades is like, both for those who die as believers as well as those who die as unbelievers.

Christ described the radically different destinies of a believer and unbeliever. So far we have learned that death has two faces: to the unbeliever the very thought of death is terrifying, or at least it should be. But for those who have made their peace with God, death is a blissful eternity.

ENGAGING THE TOPIC

Answer these questions while watching the DVD and reading the book.

1. The fall of man in the garden of Eden, and its consequence of death, was the result of Adam and Eve's _____ to God.

2. An important Old Testament word that sheds some light on the afterlife is the Hebrew word

   _____ .

3. New Testament discussion centering on the Greek word _____ provides even more clarity regarding the afterlife.

4. Today when believers die, they are said to go directly to

   _____ .

5. A tradition in medieval times was the faulty theology of

   _____ .

6. For the unbeliever, the thought of death can be

   _____ .

7. For the believer, death is a means of

   _____ .

QUESTIONS FOR DISCUSSION

1. Have you attended funerals of both believers and non-believers? If so, did you note differences between the services?

2. Read the story Jesus told in Luke 16:16–31. Have each member of the group comment on a particular characteristic of the account that stood out for them. What did you collectively learn about *hades* in this passage?

3. For a moment assume the role of Lazarus and describe the emotions he experienced; then do the same with the rich man. Consider the importance of this story for understanding the hereafter.

4. From this story, observe the reversal of roles between the rich man and Lazarus. In what ways did the rich man's perspective change after arriving in hades?

5. Focus on Luke 16:31. In what way is the statement of this man even more relevant to us than it was back in Jesus' day?

6. What is the doctrine of purgatory? Why is it faulty theology?

7. In the lecture, a sharp distinction is made between the judgment of believers and that of unbelievers. As you contemplate these passages, what does all this mean for you?

8. How would you advise someone who fears death?

PERSONAL REFLECTION

The psalmist confidently exclaims, "I am continually with you; you hold my right hand. You guide me with your counsel, and afterward you will receive me to glory. Whom have I in heaven but you? And there is nothing on earth that I desire besides you" (Psalm 73:23–25). All Christians can embrace this same confidence.

The believer is not destined for hades but rather for heaven. When we leave our earthly bodies, we will find ourselves "at home with the Lord" (2 Corinthians 5:8). Regardless of our struggles and pressures, as believers we may stand firm on the evidence of our risen Savior. As the apostle Paul wrote to Timothy, "Remember Jesus Christ, risen from the dead" (2 Timothy 2:8).

Perhaps one of the most important passages on how believers should approach death is found in Philippians 1:19–26. Here Paul said that for him to die was not a loss but a "gain." To be with Christ was "far better." This kind of faith was so prevalent among the early believers that the pagans said, "The Christians carry their dead as if in triumph!" May that be true of us also.

How forward-looking are you?

ENGAGING THE TOPIC answers:

1. Disobedience 2. Sheol 3. Hades 4. Heaven
5. Purgatory 6. Terrifying 7. Deliverance

WHAT DO BELIEVERS EXPERIENCE WHEN THEY DIE?

In preparation for these discussion questions and the DVD lecture, **please read:** | **CHAPTER 3**, *"Ascent into Glory"*

From the Author

The doctor has just told you news that you thought could only be true about someone else. You have a rare form of cancer, which almost certainly is terminal. The surgeon tells you that you have at most a year to live.

No doubt you will vacillate between despair and hope, denial and determination. Perhaps you will have more concern for those you leave behind than you do for yourself. Not a one of us can predict how we might react when it is our turn to hear the dreadful news.

And yet the Bible presents an entirely different view of

death that should give us hope. After Adam and Eve sinned, they died spiritually as well as physically. Thus God prevented Adam and Eve from eternal sinfulness by giving them the gift of death, the ability to exit this life and arrive safely in the wondrous life to come.

And why should we fear death if it is the route to our final home? Jesus assures us that there is nothing to fear; in fact, the knowledge that we shall die gives us the courage and hope to live triumphantly in this world!

ENGAGING THE TOPIC

Answer these questions while watching the DVD and reading the book.

1. The biblical view of death is one that should give the believer _____ .

2. After sinning in the garden of Eden, Adam and Eve died _____ as well as physically.

3. On the Mount of Transfiguration, Jesus described death as an _____ .

4. Our present body is a temporary structure like a _____ , where our spirit dwells.

5. Sleep is a New Testament picture of death, because the body sleeps until the day of our _____ .

6. _____ grief is grief that enables us to make the transition to a new phase of existence.

7. We should not view death as taking us from our home; rather, we should view it as _____ us into our home.

8. Christ has prepared for every believer a _____ in heaven.

QUESTIONS FOR DISCUSSION

1. Put yourself in the place of Adam or Eve. Given the same scenario, how do you think you would have responded to the same temptation they faced?

2. Do you have a loved one or friend who is facing a cancer or some other kind of terminal condition? How can you help them face this difficult transition?

3. How does the experience of Stephen help us anticipate what we will see when we arrive in heaven? (See Acts 7:54–60.)

4. Jesus often referred to death as "sleep." (Read Luke 8:52; John 11:11; and 1 Corinthians 15:52.) What did He mean by referring to death as "a sleep"? In what ways did Jesus apply that image?

5. Define "good grief." What does this kind of grief enable us to do?

6. Read Hebrew 6:19–20. What encouragements does this passage give to the believer who is anticipating heaven?

7. What kinds of investments have you made in this life that you consider valuable? What investments have you made in preparation for the life to come?

8. What does Hebrews 2:14–15 teach us? Discuss the difference between the *power* of death and the *fear* of death. How can Satan use the fear of death as a weapon against believers?

9. The apostle Paul uses an interesting image for death— that of a sailing ship weighing anchor (Philippians 1:23). Why was Paul so confident that death would be "far better"?

PERSONAL REFLECTION

Have you ever taken the pulse of your heart's desire for heaven? Once again I want you to think about Paul's words in Philippians, where the apostle Paul said, "My desire is to depart and be with Christ, for that is far better" (Philippians 1:23). Clearly, Paul had weighed the two, and there was no doubt in his mind. As we take an inventory of God's promises pertaining to heaven, we can only imagine what will be "far better."

When we do ascend into glory, consider the promise we have from our Lord regarding our final, permanent home! Jesus told us, "In my Father's house are many rooms. If it were not so, would I have told you that I go to prepare a place for you? And if I go and prepare a place for you, I will come again and will take you to myself, that where I am you may be also" (John 14:2–3). As children of God, the more we contemplate our heavenly home, the more we find that our earthly home loses its appeal.

As we await our future ascent into heaven, let us lay hold of this hope given to us in Hebrews 6:19–20: "We have this as a sure and steadfast anchor of the soul, a hope that enters into the inner place behind the curtain, where Jesus has gone as a forerunner on our behalf." Our anchor is fastened to Jesus Christ Himself!

When I asked my mother whether or nor she was sure of heaven, she replied, "I am as sure as if I am there already!" Consider where such assurance comes from and how you and I can share the same confidence.

ENGAGING THE TOPIC answers:

1. Comfort 2. Spiritually 3. Exodus 4. Tent
5. Resurrection 6. Good 7. Receiving 8. Dwelling place

WHAT CHANGES AND WHAT REMAINS THE SAME AFTER WE DIE?

In preparation for these discussion questions and the DVD lecture, **please read:**

CHAPTER 4: *"Welcome! You Have Arrived!"*

From the Author

Since we are Christ's sheep, He calls us by name, perhaps standing even as He did for Stephen. We look into His eyes and see compassion, love, and understanding. Though we are unworthy, we know His welcome is genuine.

So much is different, yet you are the same person you were while on earth. You have entered heaven without a break in consciousness. Back on earth your friends will bury your body, but they cannot bury you. Personhood survives the death of the body.

Death, someone has said, is "powerful business," for you

27

just keep living somewhere else without undue interruption. One minute after we die, our minds, our memories, will be clearer than ever before. Think of your purest joy on earth; then multiply that many times and you might catch a glimpse of heaven's euphoria.

Knowledge, love, feelings, a desire for justice—all of these are the present experience of those who have gone ahead of us to heaven. Remember that the entire personality simply carries over into the life beyond. Heaven has its differences, but it is populated with your friends, who are still the same people who once dwelt on the earth.

Death rescues us from the endlessness of this existence; it is the means by which those who love God finally are brought to Him. Only on this side of the curtain is death our enemy. Just beyond the curtain the monster turns out to be our friend.

ENGAGING THE TOPIC

Answer these questions while watching the DVD and reading the book.

1. Although we will undergo a transition from this earthly realm to the heavenly realm, our _____ will continue.

2. In heaven, _____ will no longer be part of our being.

3. In heaven our faith will give way to _____ .

4. For the believer in Christ, death is not our enemy but rather our _____ .

5. With regard to our allotted time on earth, it is not how long we live but the _____ we make that matters.

6. Our future body in heaven will be like Christ's _____ body.

QUESTIONS FOR DISCUSSION

1. What sort of welcome do you anticipate receiving upon your arrival in heaven? What kind of reunions can you envision?

2. If those in heaven you know could talk to you, what do you think they would say? If you could talk to them, what would be your first question?

3. Theologians have questions about our intermediate state—the time between our arrival in heaven and when we receive our permanent, resurrected bodies. Read 2 Corinthians 5:1 and discuss what Paul was anticipating when he died. Of what can we be certain when we arrive in heaven?

4. How does Revelation 6:9–10 help us in understanding what the saints in heaven are like today, in their appearance, ability to communicate, etc.?

5. The Bible tells us that there will be sorrow in heaven until God wipes away our tears (Revelation 7:17; 21:4). What do you think will cause our tears, both individually and collectively?

6. Discuss the topic of infant death. Consider the information both in the lecture and the book regarding this topic. Have you lost a child and do you feel free to share your experience with the group?

7. In speaking of our future state, the apostle Paul comments, "For now we see in a mirror dimly, but then face to face. Now I know in part; then I shall know fully, even as I have been fully known" (1 Corinthians 13:12). What does that verse mean to you as a believer in Christ?

PERSONAL REFLECTION

To be ushered and welcomed into heaven by our Lord will certainly eclipse any experience we had while on earth. Take a moment to envision what that will be like. What surprises might there be?

We know that our bodies in their current weak, decaying state could not withstand heaven. Whatever limitations we experience today due to our earthly body, we can rejoice that we will one day shed those limitations and enjoy a body incorruptible.

In describing our future resurrection body, the apostle Paul says, "So is it with the resurrection of the dead. What is sown is perishable; what is raised is imperishable. It is sown in dishonor; it is raised in glory. It is sown in weakness; it is raised in power. It is sown a natural body; it is raised a spiritual body. If there is a natural body, there is also a spiritual body" (1 Corinthians 15:42–44). What a glorious gift from God!

While we await the glorious event of our arrival into heaven, we must obediently continue to live our lives for the cause of Christ and joyfully endure whatever sufferings come our way. As Paul put it in his letter to the believers in Rome: "For I consider that the sufferings of this present time are not worth comparing with the glory that is to be revealed to us" (Romans 8:18).

One day we will realize this assurance Jesus gave us: "And if I go and prepare a place for you, I will come again and will take you to myself, that where I am you may be also" (John 14:3).

ENGAGING THE TOPIC answers:

1. Personalities 2. Sin 3. Sight 4. Friend 5. Contribution
6. Resurrection

DO WE REALLY HAVE TO BELIEVE IN HELL?

In preparation for these discussion questions and the DVD lecture, please read:

CHAPTER 6, *"When Hades Is Thrown into Hell"*

From the Author

Admittedly, hell is an unpleasant topic. Non-Christians disbelieve in it; most Christians ignore it. Even the staunchly biblical diehards are often silent out of embarrassment. Hell, more than any doctrine of the Bible, seems to be out of step with our times.

This doctrine is often neglected because it is difficult to reconcile with the love of God. That millions of people will be in conscious torment forever is beyond the grasp of the human mind. To put it simply, to us the punishment of hell does not fit the crime. Yes, all men do some evil and a few do great evils, but nothing that anyone has done can justify eternal torment.

At the root of the debate is the question of whether hell is fair and just. To us humans, everlasting punishment is disproportionate to the offense committed. God appears cruel, unjust, sadistic, and vindictive. The purpose of punishment, we are told, is always redemptive. The concept of a place where there will be endless punishment without any possibility of parole or reform seems unjust.

We must confess that we do not know exactly how much punishment is enough for those who have sinned against God. We may think we know what God is like, but we see through a glass darkly.

What if, from God's point of view, the greatness of sin is determined by the greatness of the One against whom it is committed? Then the guilt of sin is infinite because it is a violation of the character of an infinite being. What if, in the nature of God, it is deemed that such infinite sins deserve an infinite penalty, a penalty that no one can ever pay?

We read that in the final judgment the unbelieving dead of all ages stand before God to be judged. But after the judgment, hades is thrown into the lake of fire. Yet, there is no doubt that some of the characteristics of hades continue, or more accurately, that the suffering of hades is intensified in hell.

ENGAGING THE TOPIC

Answer these questions while watching the DVD and reading the book.

1. People often neglect the doctrine of hell because it is difficult to reconcile with the _____ of God.

2. _____ is the name given to the belief that eventually all people will arrive safely to heaven.

3. Conditional _____ contends that all people will not be saved, but neither will any be in conscious torment forever.

4. At the root of the debate on hell is whether it is fair and _____ .

5. According to Acts 4:12, a _____ knowledge of Christ is required for one's salvation.

6. Those who believe in Christ will receive mercy. Those who do not will receive _____ .

7. Although hell has an access, it has no _____ .

QUESTIONS FOR DISCUSSION

1. Many people, especially unbelievers, have a skeptical or even flippant view of hell. Discuss some of the common reasons people claim they do not believe in hell. Members of the group may be able to share some conversations they have had with others who expressed their cynicism or skepticism.

2. Discuss the basic idea of the theory of *universalism*. What are its weaknesses from a biblical point of view?

3. Another alternate teaching to the doctrine of hell is *conditional immortality*. What are the tenets of this teaching? According to Scripture, where does it fall short?

4. What will God base His judgment of people on? (See Revelation 20:12–13.) Should we interpret this to mean that people can enter heaven based on their good works? (Please note that good works are a basis for judgment, but not the basis of salvation.)

5. According to Scripture, why is a personal knowledge of Christ needed for one's salvation?

6. What is the relationship between God's holiness and the existence of hell?

7. The Greek language of the New Testament uses three words to describe hell: *tartarus*, *gehenna*, and *hades*. What is unique about each term, and what does each contribute to our understanding of the New Testament concept of hell?

8. As we learn from this chapter, hell has several characteristics. Discuss briefly each of those characteristics.

9. As finite, created beings, are we able to totally grasp the concept of eternity? Take turns discussing your understanding of eternity. Relate the concept of eternity also to the existence of heaven.

PERSONAL REFLECTION

There will be a day of judgment and final sentencing for those who rejected God and His gift of salvation. As we read in Revelation 20:12, "And I saw the dead, great and small, standing before the throne, and books were opened. Then another book was opened, which is the book of life. And the dead were judged by what was written in the books, according to what they had done." For the unbeliever, what a sobering day that will be.

Scripture teaches us that hell is a very real place. It is a place of final death and final destiny for those who do not know Jesus Christ as their personal Savior. "Then Death and Hades were thrown into the lake of fire. This is the second death, the lake of fire. And if anyone's name was not found written in the book of life, he was thrown into the lake of fire" (Revelation 20:14–15). It is always appropriate for God's children to praise God and thank Him for His gift of salvation. How often do you take the time to express praise to God?

Contemplate how God's gracious gift of salvation is received: "And there is salvation in no one else, for there is no other name under heaven given among men by which we must be saved" (Acts 4:12). "Whoever believes in the Son has eternal life; whoever does not obey the Son shall not see life, but the wrath of God remains on him" (John 3:36). Do you make it a point to be a witness in your daily walk? When you meet others who are at the crossroads of their lives and searching for an answer, are you ready to share the gospel?

ENGAGING THE TOPIC answers:

1. Love 2. Universalism 3. Immortality 4. Just 5. Personal 6. Justice 7. Exit

WHAT WILL OUR RESURRECTION BODY BE LIKE?

In preparation for these discussion questions and the DVD lecture, please read:	**CHAPTER FOUR**, *"Welcome! You Have Arrived!"*

From the Author

We need to understand what our future, resurrection bodies will be like. This is critical, because in the minds of most Christians, the eternal state is going to be an ethereal, distant, spirit-like kind of existence that has no connection with this earth or who they are on this planet. In this study, I am going to stress the *continuity* between this world and the next, not the radical differences.

Keep in mind that you were created and designed to live on this earth. And as a believer, after you die, you will continue to live on a re-created and redeemed earth.

When man fell, creation fell. And now creation is eagerly awaiting our redemption, because it cannot be redeemed until we are. Until our redemption, the curse of sin will always hang over nature. Our redemption and the resurrection of the body are very important.

Your resurrection body will have continuity with the body you have now. Take a good look in the mirror, and realize that your new body is going to be something like the one you see. I fully expect to recognize you in heaven, even though you will be remade. It is important to understand the continuity of our bodies between this life and the next.

The Bible tells us in Philippians 3:21 that the Lord Jesus Christ "will transform our lowly body to be like his glorious body." That gives us total permission to look at the resurrected body of Jesus and say that is how our resurrected bodies will be. In addition, 1 John 3:2 says that "when he appears we shall be like him, because we shall see him as he is." We shall bear the likeness of Jesus. How much clearer could the Bible be that our bodies are going to be like the body of the resurrected Jesus!

When Adam sinned, the entire creation was somehow infected with sin. When man fell, creation fell. And now creation is eagerly awaiting our redemption, because it cannot be redeemed until we are. Until our redemption, the curse of sin will always hang over nature. Our redemption and the resurrection of the body are very important.

Christians in Paul's day expected to live until Jesus returned. But when Jesus didn't return and their friends and relatives were dying, the living believers wondered whether they would be reunited again. Paul taught that when Jesus returns, the spirits of believers who have died will return with Jesus and they will be joined with their resurrected bodies at that time. Then, we who are still alive will be caught up together with them with our resurrection bodies and "we will be together with the Lord."

Resurrection is so important because it shows the triumph of God over the material world and the reconciliation of God in the re-created earth.

ENGAGING THE TOPIC

Answer these questions while watching the DVD and reading the book.

1. When Adam sinned, the entire creation was _____ with sin.

2. Creation will remain under the curse of sin until our _____.

3. Our current bodies are sown in _____ but raised _____.

4. When Jesus met with the disciples in His resurrected body, He continued to build on _____ relationships.

5. When Jesus returns to resurrect believers, the dead in Christ will rise _____ .

6. Our resurrected bodies will be like _____ resurrected body.

QUESTIONS FOR DISCUSSION

1. Discuss Romans 8:18–26. Why does creation "groan"?
Why is resurrection so important? How will our redemption change the order of things in nature?

2. Have you ever wondered exactly what your resurrected
body will look like? Read Luke 24:36–43. Take note of
the characteristics of Jesus' resurrected body. What can
we learn from this passage regarding what our resurrected bodies will be like?

3. Discuss points of similarity and differences between
the body we have now and the one we will have based on
1 Corinthians 15:42–44.

4. Again think about a question posed in a previous lecture: Those in heaven today do not yet have their resurrected bodies, so how do they function?

5. First John 3:2 tells us that we shall see Jesus "as he is." Think about what Christ was able to do after He was raised from the dead. What does that passage mean to the believer in Christ?

6. After His resurrection, Jesus reconnected with His disciples and friends He had before His death. Discuss what joy it will be to resume friendships and relationships with those who have gone on to heaven before us.

7. Read 1 Thessalonians 4:13–18. When Christ returns, believers will be resurrected. How does Scripture describe this event?

8. What does the fact of the resurrection show the world?

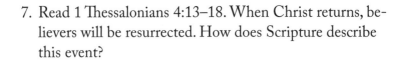

PERSONAL REFLECTION

One day we will receive a new, resurrection body that will serve us for eternity. "So is it with the resurrection of the dead. What is sown is perishable; what is raised is imperishable. It is sown in dishonor; it is raised in glory. It is sown in weakness; it is raised in power. It is sown a natural body; it is raised a spiritual body" (1 Corinthians 15:42–44).

First John 3:2 tells us even more about our resurrection body. "Beloved, we are God's children now, and what we will be has not yet appeared; but we know that when he appears we shall be like him, because we shall see him as he is." This is a most encouraging passage of Scripture. Not only does it promise that we will finally see Jesus in all His glory, but it also gives us wonderful insight into what our resurrected bodies will be like.

Do you often give thought to Jesus' return? First Thessalonians 4:13–18 has been a great encouragement to believers since Jesus' resurrection. "We do not want you to be uninformed, brothers, about those who are asleep, that you may not grieve as others do who have no hope. For since we believe that Jesus died and rose again, even so, through Jesus, God will bring with him those who have fallen asleep. For this we declare to you by a word from the Lord, that we who are alive, who are left until the coming of the Lord, will not precede those who have fallen asleep. For the Lord himself will descend from heaven with a cry of command, with the voice of an archangel, and with the sound of the trumpet of God. And the dead in Christ will rise first. Then we who are alive, who are left, will be caught up together with them in the clouds to meet the Lord in the air, and so we will always be with the Lord. Therefore encourage one another with these words."

ENGAGING THE TOPIC answers:

1. Infected 2. Redemption 3. Dishonor, imperishable
4. Past 5. First 6. Jesus'

HOW DIFFERENT WILL HEAVEN BE?

In preparation for these discussion questions and the DVD lecture, please read: | **CHAPTER 5,** *"Living in the New Jerusalem"*

From the Author

We've already emphasized that we will make the transition into heaven without a break in consciousness. Those whom you did not know on earth are just as instantly known as those of your earthly friends who often joined you at your favorite restaurant. Your uncle asks you about the well-being of some of his relatives, but the primary conversation is about the beauty of Christ, the wonder of God's love, and the undeserved grace that makes you a beneficiary of such blessings.

At your leisure you explore your new home. This, after all, is where you will spend eternity, so it is worth a look. This new city came out of heaven since it is part of the heavenly realm. We will have a number of special privileges such as worshipping God and serving the Most High in whatever capacity is assigned to us.

If we want to prepare for our final destination, we should begin to worship God here on earth. Our arrival in heaven will only be a continuation of what we already have begun. Praise is the language of heaven and the language of the faithful on earth.

Having seen heaven, we will find that earth has lost all its attractions. We only wish that those we left behind would know how important it was to be faithful to Christ. Looked at from the other side of the curtain, knowing what is now so clear to us, we wish we could shout to earth encouraging believers to serve Christ with all their hearts. We wish we had grasped this before the call came for us to come up higher.

We weep as we think of all the people still on earth who most probably will not be joining us. We know that we would weep forever except that God comes to wipe the tears from our eyes.

ENGAGING THE TOPIC

Answer these questions while watching the DVD and reading the book.

1. After our arrival in heaven, our primary conversation will be about the beauty of _____ .

2. Admittance into the New Jerusalem will only be for those whose names are written in the Lamb's Book of

_____ .

3. The dimensions of the new city will be fifteen hundred
   _____ square.

4. In the New Jerusalem, each child of God will have his
   and her own _____ .

5. Activity around the throne of God is uninhibited
   _____ and spontaneous _____ .

6. In heaven, _____ , which is the result
   of sin, is banished forever.

QUESTIONS FOR DISCUSSION

1. Read Revelation 21 and make a list of all the things that
   "won't be" in heaven.

2. Read Revelation 21:16 and note the dimensions of the
   city. Because much of the details are left to our specula-
   tion, spend a moment to imagine what the living condi-
   tions will be like and how you will connect with others.

3. Read Revelation 4:5, the description of the throne of God. (See also 19:5–6.) Describe the scene you picture in your mind's eye.

4. Contrast our present access to God with the access we will have in the New Jerusalem.

5. We've considered this before but again we must ask: What if when you arrive in heaven, some of your relatives or friends are not present? How difficult will it be for you to manage your sorrow until God wipes the tears from our eyes? Do you expect to have regrets?

6. Pause a few moments to consider what we, as believers, can do to encourage others to take advantage of the salvation Jesus offers. Based on your group discussion, what might be on your "To-Do" action list?

PERSONAL REFLECTION

Revelation 21:1–2 gives us a quick snapshot of our new future home: "Then I saw a new heaven and a new earth, for the first heaven and the first earth had passed away, and the sea was no more. And I saw the holy city, new Jerusalem, coming down out of heaven from God, prepared as a bride adorned for her husband." Originating in heaven, this city is a new creation bringing with it a new order of reality. Its inhabitants are the children of God.

It appears that the predominant activities in the New Jerusalem will be the praise and worship of God. John describes the scene at the throne of God, "And from the throne came a voice saying, 'Praise our God, all you his servants, you who fear him, small and great.' Then I heard what seemed to be the voice of a great multitude, like the roar of many waters and like the sound of mighty peals of thunder, crying out, 'Hallelujah! For the Lord our God the Almighty reigns'" (Revelation 19:5–6).

It seems that we often get too caught up in the duties of our earthly existence to reflect on our future destination. Our step beyond the curtain to the other side could be years down the road, or it could come at any moment. Perhaps one way we might prepare for heaven is to take the time for praising our Lord and Savior for who He is and what He has done for us. How else might we prepare ourselves while on earth for our new home?

"As my dad lay dying, he was still conscious on earth but it already seemed as if he was spending time in heaven," a young woman said. How can we "spend time in heaven" before our actual arrival?

ENGAGING THE TOPIC answers:

1. Christ 2. Life 3. Miles 4. Dwelling place
5. Praise, worship 6. Pain

DVD SECTION 8

WHAT WILL THE NEW JERUSALEM BE LIKE?

In preparation for these discussion questions and the DVD lecture, **please read:**

CHAPTER 5, *"Living in the New Jerusalem"* *(reread this chapter as review)*

CHAPTER 7, *"When the Curtain Opens for You"*

CHAPTER 8, *"Knowing Today Where You Will Be Tomorrow"*

From the Author

We can scarcely comprehend the details of the New Jerusalem, a city that strains our imagination. On the twelve gates of the city were written the names of the twelve tribes of Israel, which indicates that many rooms will be taken up by the saints of the Old Testament. The wall of the city has twelve foundation stones. The foundation stones represent the New Testament saints. Both Old and New Testament believers are there.

The Bible tells us that the streets of heaven are paved with gold. The wall around the city is made of jasper. And the twelve gates are made of twelve pearls, each gate made of a single pearl. We ask, is all this literal? Either way, these descriptions represent something even more beautiful than precious stones could ever be.

We think that heaven is going to be so different, but look at the similarities. The city has walls and gates and streets. It has a water source. It has the Tree of Life. It also has travel, communication, beauty, and architecture. The nations will continue to exist. This is indeed heaven on earth!

Why is the city so beautiful? It was John Piper who said that nobody goes to the Grand Canyon to get a better self-image of one's self. You go to the Grand Canyon to adore the wonder of what someone else has created. As you observe it, you begin to adore God. In the same way, the New Jerusalem exists that we may become overwhelmed with its beauty, its strength, and its grandeur.

Heaven is going to be a place of eternal creativity and service. We will continue many of the same activities we have here, and in doing so we will serve Him. Jonathan Edwards said that the ideas of God go on for all of eternity. For all of eternity, we are going to be learning more about God. The Bible says that when we trust Christ as Savior, we inherit "all things." That means that we get all of God. And we get all of the New Jerusalem. We will have open access to all that God has to offer us.

When believers die, they die within the assurance of God's love. God loves you as His child in ways beyond what we can describe. Believers also die within the circle of God's providence. When you trust Christ as Savior, He takes you all the way home, no matter how you die.

ENGAGING THE TOPIC

Answer these questions while watching the DVD and reading the book.

1. The twelve gates of the city represent the believers of the
   _____.

2. The twelve foundation stones represent the believers of
   the _____ .

3. One of our primary occupations in heaven will be to
   _____ God.

4. Although Adam and Eve could not eat of the Tree of
   _____, in heaven we may eat freely of it.

5. When it comes time to die, believers may be confident
   that they will die within the _____ of
   God's love.

6. Throughout eternity we will increase our
   _____ of God and His wondrous works.

QUESTIONS FOR DISCUSSION

1. The New Jerusalem has twelve gates and twelve foundation stones. Remind yourself of what these symbolize.
   (See Revelation 21:12–14.)

2. Why do you believe God adorns the city with such beauty? Do you see any correlation or continuity with the beauty and grandeur we see in God's creation this side of heaven?

3. What is the marriage supper of the Lamb? At the marriage supper, on what basis will we be clothed? (See Revelation 19:6–10.)

4. Scripture tells us that the holy city will be interpenetrated with light from God Himself (Revelation 22:5). Could this be the same kind of light from which God needed to shield Moses in the Old Testament?

5. What does the "family of God" in heaven entail? Discuss Jesus' point in Mark 3:33–35.

6. Based on your reading of chapter 7 of the book, "When the Curtain Opens for You," discuss how and why Jesus is our best example of how to face death. (See also Matthew 26:38, 42; Luke 23:46.)

7. Based on your reading of chapter 8, "Knowing Today Where You Will Be Tomorrow," discuss how one can be sure of being welcomed into heaven at death.

8. Given what we know about heaven from God's Word, what is our responsibility here and now to our neighbors and friends regarding eternity?

PERSONAL REFLECTION

What a blessing to know that, as believers, we die within the assurance of God's love, and that we die within the circle of His providence. We will most likely be surprised, even stunned by what we see when we enter heaven. "As it is written, 'What no eye has seen, nor ear heard, nor the heart of man imagined, what God has prepared for those who love him'" (1 Corinthians 2:9).

Heaven will truly be a place for the extended family of God. Jesus said, "For whoever does the will of God, he is my brother and sister and mother" (Mark 3:35). Not only may we anticipate reuniting with our own earthly family members who have gone to heaven before us, we will be enriched throughout eternity by being part of the greater family of God. What joy it will be to get to know so many others who also love Jesus!

While he was being crucified next to Jesus, the thief placed his trust in Jesus as his Savior. Our Lord's response, "Truly, I say to you, today you will be with me in Paradise"

(Luke 23:43), was a promise the thief carried with himself to heaven a very short time later. When we trust Christ as Savior, we may go through times of doubt—whether we are new believers or "seasoned saints." But at the end of the day, we can rest assured on the promises of Jesus.

"Today you will be with me in Paradise."

ENGAGING THE TOPIC answers:

1. Old Testament 2. New Testament 3. Worship 4. Life
5. Assurance 6. Knowledge

MORE **ONE MINUTE AFTER YOU DIE** PRODUCTS

More than 700,000 in print!

ONE MINUTE AFTER YOU DIE

ERWIN W. LUTZE

- Book
- DVD

DVD

ONE MINUTE AFTER YOU DIE

ERWIN W. LUTZER

MORE BOOKS BY
ERWIN W. LUTZER

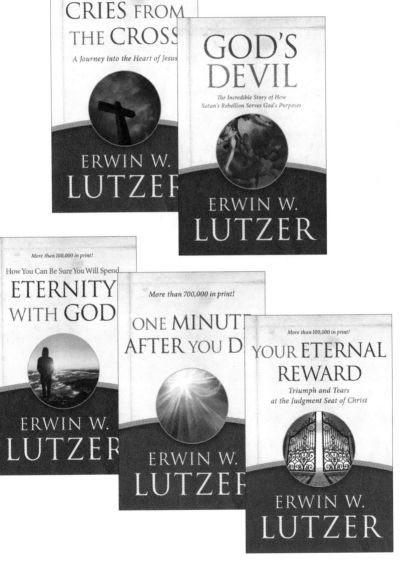

CRIES FROM THE CROSS
A Journey into the Heart of Jesus

ERWIN W. LUTZER

GOD'S DEVIL
The Incredible Story of How
Satan's Rebellion Serves God's Purposes

ERWIN W. LUTZER

More than 100,000 in print!
How You Can Be Sure You Will Spend
ETERNITY WITH GOD

ERWIN W. LUTZER

More than 700,000 in print!
ONE MINUTE AFTER YOU D...

ERWIN W. LUTZER

More than 100,000 in print!
YOUR ETERNAL REWARD
*Triumph and Tears
at the Judgment Seat of Christ*

ERWIN W. LUTZER

MOODY Publishers™

From the Word to Life